ONLINE ENTREPRENEURSHIP

SERIES:

WEALTH 2022

ONLINE ENTREPRENEURSHIP

Series "Wealth 2022"
By: D.K. Hawkins
Version 1.1 ~December 2021
Published by D.K. Hawkins at KDP
Copyright ©2021 by D.K. Hawkins. All rights reserved.

No part of this publication may be reproduced, distributed or transmitted in any form or by any means including photocopying, recording or other electronic or mechanical methods or by any information storage or retrieval system without the prior written permission of the publishers, except in the case of very brief quotations embodied in critical reviews and certain other noncommercial uses permitted by copyright law.

All rights reserved, including the right of reproduction in whole or in part in any form.

All information in this book has been carefully researched and checked for factual accuracy. However, the author and publisher make no warranty, express or implied, that the information contained herein is appropriate for every individual, situation, or purpose and assume no responsibility for errors or omissions.

The reader assumes the risk and full responsibility for all actions. The author will not be held responsible for any loss or damage, whether consequential, incidental, special, or otherwise, that may result from the information presented in this book.

All images are free for use or purchased from stock photo sites or royalty-free for commercial use. I have relied on my own observations as well as many different sources for this book, and I have done my best to check facts and give credit where it is due. In the event that any material is used without proper permission, please contact me so that the oversight can be corrected.

The information provided in this book is for informational purposes only and is not intended to be a source of advice or credit analysis with respect to the material presented. The information and/or documents contained in this book do not constitute legal or financial advice and should never be used without first consulting with a financial professional to determine what may be best for your individual needs.

The publisher and the author do not make any guarantee or other promise as to any results that may be obtained from using the content of this book. You should never make any investment decision without first consulting with your own financial advisor and conducting your own research and due diligence. To the maximum extent permitted by law, the publisher and the author disclaim any and all liability in the event any information, commentary, analysis, opinions, advice and/or recommendations contained in this book prove to be inaccurate, incomplete, or unreliable or result in any investment or other losses.

Content contained or made available through this book is not intended to and does not constitute legal advice or investment advice, and no attorney-client relationship is formed. The publisher and the author are providing this book and its contents on an "as is" basis. Your use of the information in this book is at your own risk.

Contents

Introduction: 7
Chapter no.1 9
Introduction to online entrepreneurship. 9
What is an online entrepreneur? 9
What does an online entrepreneur do? 10
Tips for young entrepreneurs. 10
Chapter no.2 18
How to Become an online entrepreneur. 18
Ensure Financial Stability. 19
Build a Diverse Skill Set. 19
Consume Content Across Multiple Channels. 20
Identify a Problem to Solve. 21
Solve That Problem. 21
Network Like Crazy. 22
Lead by Example. 22
Entrepreneurship Financing. 23
Resources for Entrepreneurs. 23
Chapter no.3 26
Characteristics of online Entrepreneurs. 26
1. **Versatile.** 27
2. **Flexible.** 28
   3. Money Savvy. 29
   4. Resilient. 29

- 5. Focused. 30
- 6. Business Smart. 30
  - 7. Communicators. 31
- How Entrepreneurship Helps Economies. 33
- Chapter no.4 35
- How to become an online entrepreneur. 35
- Online entrepreneur skills. 38
- Salary and job outlook for online entrepreneurs. 41
- Chapter no.5 42
- Successful Online Entrepreneur. 42
- • Understand You're "Why" 43
- • Don't Leave Your Full-Time Job…yet. 43
- 2. Business Idea That Fits Your Lifestyle. 44
- • Learn While You Go 47
- • Get Started Now. 48
- • Create a Plan and stick to It. 49
- • Do your best to work hard. 49
- • Don't be afraid to experiment with the new stuff. 50
- • Make Short-Term Goals. 50
- • Don't be afraid to decide to invest. 51
- • Reinvest Profits from Your Business. 51
- Chapter no.6 53
- Become an entrepreneur without money and experience. 53
- How to Become an entrepreneur. 53

4. Create something superior (or less expensive) than what's available. 57

6. Begin with a minimum-viable production (MVP). 59

7. Develop a business strategy. 60

How to find a Founder or Co-Founder. 63

How to Get Funding. 64

7. You can get a microloan. 66

How to incorporate your business. 67

The Benefits of incorporating. 67

The disadvantages of incorporating. 68

Entrepreneur Help & Support. 68

Support Networks. 71

Chapter no.7 73

Drawbacks & Benefits of Online Business. 73

What is Online Business? 73

Benefits from Online Business 73

The disadvantages of online Business. 78

Differences Between E-Business and Traditional Business. ..81

Chapter no.8 84

Understand Operating an Online Business. 84

Create a Clear Business Vision. 86

Create the Business Plan. 87

Create The Store You Want to Create Online Store. 88

Promote Your Online Lingerie Business. 90

The E-Business Risks. 90

Questions for Entrepreneurs. 93
Conclusion: 96

Introduction:

Entrepreneurship is the process of starting a business. Entrepreneurs are usually pioneers and innovators of innovative ideas, product solutions, or business procedures. Entrepreneurs are essential to the economy as they have the capability and the ability to anticipate requirements and bring innovative ideas to the market. Entrepreneurs create a new business, face the most significant risk, and reap the greatest rewards. The entrepreneur who succeeds in embracing the risk of starting a company will be rewarded with money, fame, recognition, and the potential for continuous expansion. Failure by an entrepreneur can result in losses and less visibility in the marketplace for those involved.

- An entrepreneur makes a new business endeavor.
- An entrepreneur develops a firm to implement their idea, which aggregates money and labor to produce goods or services for profit.
- Entrepreneurship is high-risk, but it can also be high-rewarding because it contributes to economic riches, growth, and innovation.
- For entrepreneurs, securing finance is critical: funding options include SBA loans and crowdfunding.
- The form of their business determines the method entrepreneurs file and pay taxes.

Entrepreneurship is one of the four resources economics defines as production requires: land/natural resources, labor, and capital. To develop things or supply services, an entrepreneur combines the first three of them. They usually design a company strategy, recruit staff, acquire resources and finance, and supervise its operations.

The words "entrepreneur," as well as "entrepreneurship," have not been defined uniformly by economists (the term "entrepreneur" is derived from the French verb entreprendre, which means "to take on"). Even though an entrepreneur's idea has been around since the beginning, classical and neoclassical economists did not include entrepreneurs in their formal models because they assumed that perfectly rational people would have all the information, leaving no room to take risks or discover. The economists didn't attempt to include entrepreneurship in their models until around the mid-century of the 20th century. Entrepreneurs were included due to three thought leaders: Joseph Schumpeter, Frank Knight, and Israel Kirzner. In pursuit of profit, Schumpeter claimed entrepreneurs, not only businesses, were responsible for inventing new products. Knight said they were the ones who were the bearers of uncertainty and were responsible for the risk-adjusted prices in the financial markets. According to Kirzner, it is a procedure that results in discovery.

Chapter no.1

Introduction to online entrepreneurship.

Entrepreneurship is an intriguing ambition for many people who seek greater control over their careers and more flexibility. Through e-commerce and other digital channels, technological advancements have made this aim more accessible to enterprises of all sizes. If you're thinking about beginning your own online business, it's a good idea to understand the steps you'll need to take. This post will look at what an online entrepreneur is, what they do, how to become one, and what skills they need.

What is an online entrepreneur?

An online entrepreneur is a company owner that operates their corporation exclusively online. They, like other entrepreneurs, frequently assume financial or other personal risks to start their own business. To sell items or services, online entrepreneurs might employ a variety of business models. Here are some instances of online entrepreneurs:

- Bloggers
- Content creators
- Owners of e-commerce sites
- Online consultants

What does an online entrepreneur do?

Based on their field of work and goals in their professional lives, the day-to-day activities could include:

- Responding to emails or writing letters
- Update of website content
- Writing blogs or articles
- Contacting current and prospective clients
- Contacting vendors, such

Tips for young entrepreneurs.

Some pointers to help you succeed as a young entrepreneur:

1. Take business courses.

Take accounting, economics, or business courses while getting your high school certificate or GED. These courses will provide you with an understanding of the essentials of beginning your own business.

2. Research college programs.

Young entrepreneurs benefit from having a college degree because numerous degree programs provide substantial knowledge of starting a firm. College can also provide you with the opportunity to conduct a specialized study or complete an internship in a field of interest, allowing you to get even more business experience.

3. Watch webinars.

Webinars are an excellent way for new entrepreneurs to learn about the business world. Successful entrepreneurs frequently give webinars to provide advice and answer questions about how they got their business off the ground. Take notes when viewing webinars so you may use them as a resource when you start your own company.

4. Plan how to raise capital.

Young entrepreneurs typically work to raise money because they may not have the funds to start their business with their funds. Young entrepreneurs can raise funds for their businesses in various ways, including organizing a fundraiser, applying for a business loan, or receiving a business grant.

5. Build a budget.

Because many young entrepreneurs start their enterprises with limited cash or small loans, you must create a budget that you can stick to. You can hire someone to help you create a budget, or you can do it yourself by writing down your expenses and creating a budget. When making a budget, take the time to evaluate your costs and loan interest rates.

6. **Do work you like.**

Starting a business, you are excited about can keep you motivated to accomplish the work. For example, if you're enthusiastic about healthcare, you could create an app that links individuals to the resources and doctors they need.

7. **Believe in yourself.**

As a new entrepreneur, it's critical to have faith in your company and think it will succeed. Confident young entrepreneurs are more willing to take chances to help them succeed. It's critical to exude confidence in yourself and your company when meeting with investors and business partners with more experience than you, as this may help you get their support.

8. **Start an entrepreneur club.**

To meet other young entrepreneurs, organize an entrepreneur club at your school. You can plan activities to teach business management skills, invite speakers to provide entrepreneurship lectures, or brainstorm ideas for new company ventures.

9. Network with other young entrepreneurs.

Networking with other young entrepreneurs might help you build your company relationships and gain access to more opportunities. Make an effort to engage with as many young entrepreneurs as possible to enhance your chances of success. Join organizations and utilize social media networking platforms to network with other entrepreneurs in the same age group.

10. Research realistic timelines for growth.

It's critical to have a realistic notion of how long you'll need to expand your company. Starting a business can take a few months to several years, depending on the industry. To better understand your company's growth timetable, do some research to see how long similar companies' growth trajectories were.

11. Envision your dream business.

Consider the message you want to send, the scale of your company, and the benefits you can provide to individuals. Imagining your ideal business might assist you in determining your short- and long-term objectives. If your dream company employs more than 100 people, for example, you can set a short-term objective of recruiting ten employees in the first two years to achieve your long-term goal of hiring more.

12. Think about your ideal lifestyle.

When establishing a business as a young entrepreneur, keeping your ideal lifestyle in mind is critical. Consider significant life decisions that may impact your business, such as where you want to live, how much money you want to make, and whether or not you want to start a family.

13. Trust the process.

You may be eager for your firm to increase as a new entrepreneur. However, keep in mind that launching a business is a multi-step process, and finding money, gaining clients, and marketing your firm might take months. During the growth process, you can use any spare time to focus on your objectives and ensure that everything is functioning smoothly.

14. Write out a 10-year plan.

Writing a 10-year plan allows you to visualize your goals and define action steps to assist you in growing your business and see what you can do now to help your firm thrive in the future. Sit down and write down where you want your business to be in ten years, then create steps outlining how you'll get there.

15. Take your time.

Because businesses typically take a long time to develop, you must focus on taking your time and not rushing the process. Taking your time can help you avoid making costly mistakes and feeling stressed.

16. Build a strong team.

It's critical to surround yourself with a solid team of specialists that share your enthusiasm and determination. Surrounding yourself with a group of people who share your aims can help you be more productive and create a more positive work atmosphere. You might play various roles, such as financial advisers who manage your company's finances or marketing advisors who handle your company's marketing.

17. Learn from your mistakes.

It's natural for a new entrepreneur to make mistakes when establishing a business. Instead of becoming discouraged by your blunders, try to see them as a learning opportunity. Remember what caused the mistake, so you don't make the same mistake again.

18. Interview business owners.

Other business entrepreneurs may be able to provide you with helpful advice for starting your own company. Experienced business owners may offer anecdotes about their experiences beginning a firm, disclose mistakes they've made, explain their aims, and demonstrate the actions they followed to make their company successful.

19. Ask to shadow an entrepreneur.

Observing how a firm runs and how an entrepreneur acts daily is possible when you shadow an entrepreneur. They may demonstrate how they communicate with their coworkers, collaborate effectively with their business partners, or which skills they employ to work efficiently.

20. Start a microbusiness.

A microbusiness is a company with less than ten people who rely on fewer resources to get up and run. Starting a microbusiness can benefit young entrepreneurs since it allows them to master creating an enterprise on a smaller scale.

21. Enter contests.

Entering young entrepreneur competitions increases your confidence and allows you to demonstrate your abilities to the commercial world. You'll be able to pitch your business ideas while networking with other young entrepreneurs. Contests may give financial rewards, which you can spend toward your business, or educational incentives, such as scholarships. Look online for young entrepreneur competitions and discover if ones are a suitable fit for you.

22. Keep challenging yourself.

It's critical as a new entrepreneur to keep yourself challenged to continue growing and learning. If you're a student, push yourself by enrolling in advanced classes. If you're currently working on your company, look for additional educational tools such as books and podcasts to help you come up with new ideas.

Chapter no.2

How to Become an online entrepreneur.

Many people are enthralled by the notion of being entrepreneurs in the 21st century because of Internet companies like Alphabet, which was previously Google (GOOG), as well as Meta (FB), which was formerly Facebook and Meta (FB), each of them has helped their founders become extremely rich. Contrary to established professions, in which there's usually a specific route to follow, many people find the path to being an entrepreneur a little confusing. What works for one company owner may not be suitable for one and vice to the other. But, the majority of the successful entrepreneurs on the Internet have followed these seven basic steps:

Ensure Financial Stability.

It is not a mandatory initial step, but it is highly encouraged. While some online entrepreneurs have built successful businesses on a shoestring budget Facebook, now Meta, founder Mark Zuckerberg, starting with a sufficient cash. He also ensured that he had ongoing funding which can only benefit an aspiring entrepreneur. This will help in gving them more time to focus on building a successful business, while on the other hand, not have to worry about making quick money.

Build a Diverse Skill Set.

Once a person's finances are securly set up, it's critical to develop various talents. Then put those various skills and talents to work in the real world. Step two and step one can be comepleted together to be the most beneficial. Learning and doing new things in real-world circumstances will help you develop your particular skill set. If an ambitious online entrepreneur has a background in finance, for example, they can go into a sales function at their current company to gain the soft skills needed to succeed. When online entrepreneurs develop a varied skill set, they have a toolkit to fall back on when faced with difficult situations. Sometimes college is required to become successful entrepreneur and sometimes it is not. Some examples of those who choose not to attend college and still become successful entrepreneur is Bill Gates, Larry Ellison, Mark Zuckerberg and Steve Jobs.

Attending (and paying) for college is not required to start a successful business, it may educate young people about the world in various ways. The famous college dropouts mentioned above are the exception, not the. Still, college might not be for everyone considereding the high cost of education in the United States. It is not true that a bachelor's degree in any type of business is required before you can start your own business.People who have had successful companies have majored in various areas (even psychology), and doing so can open your eyes that can aid you in the establishment of your firm.

Consume Content Across Multiple Channels.

The need to absorb varied content is a vital area to know just like developing a diverse skill set as well. To consume contents books, articles, and podcasts are all great outlets. The point is that the information you are consuming should cover various topics regardless of where you are getting it at. Aspiring entrepreneurs should consistently acquaint themselves with the world around them. To always be looking at different sectors from new viewpoints. This will allow them to establish a business around different and specific areas.

Identify a Problem to Solve.

An ambitious online entrepreneur can identify a variety of problems to solve by watching and learning from content across many areas of media. Many people think that to be succesful your service or product needs to addess something specific and help another company or client solve it. An ambitious entrepreneur will see the need and develop his company around the issue that he has identified. Steps three and four needs to be done together in order to fix the problem by taking other industries and looking at it from the outside. This will allow an ambitious online entrepreneur to spot problems that others may miss.

Solve That Problem.

Successful startups always address a specific problem that will help other business or the public at large. It is referred to as "bringing value to the problem." The only way that an entrepreneur can be successful if they can add value to a specific problem. Let's say you see that scheduling a doctor or dentist appointment is difficult for patients. Due to this they are losing business. To solve this you build an online appointment system that could making booking appointments easier for the patient.

Network Like Crazy.

The majority of online entrepreneurs cannot succeed on their own. The business world is very cutthroat. Any and all assistance you can obtain from networking will always benefit you. For any new entrepreneur, to network is life and essential for your business. By meeting the proper individuals who can then connect you with other industry contacts such as suppliers, funders, and even mentors can possibly mean the difference between your success and failure. Also, attend conferences, emailing and contacting industry contacts, and meeting with your cousin's friend's brother who works in a related field can all help you get out into the world and meet people who can help you. Once you get your foot in the door, the proper people will help you conduct your business that much faster.

Lead by Example.

For you to succeed as a great entrepreneur you must be a great leader first. Performing the day-to-day tasks in your business by yourself will not result in success. A leader must always work hard, and then motivate, and inspire their staff to achieve their full potential. This will lead to the company's success. At the most successful organizations you have great executives. For example; Steve Jobs and Apple, Disney had Bob Igor, and Bill Gates was with Microsoft. Take nots of successful individuals with successful companies. Read books that are writted about them, study their speeches. By doing this you can learn what they are doing in order to be a great leader and thereby showing your staff what a great leader that you are.

Entrepreneurship Financing.

With any new venture, entrepreneurs will find that capital funding could be hard to qualify for. Many entrepreneurs will start their company by using their own money, doing their own work to cut down the cost of labor, have very little labor and will factor in receivables. Some entrepreneurs will work by themselves to get their business up and running. Other entrepreneurs will work with established small business who can generate the money and resources that they will need. New businesses who are in search of funding might look to an angel investor, crowdfunding, venture capitalists, or hedge funds.

Resources for Entrepreneurs.

There is good news. There are different financing options available for entrepreneurs who are just starting out. The Small Business Administration (SBA) can assist entrepreneurs in launching their businesses with a low-interest business loan. The Small Business Administration (SBA) assists firms in finding loan providers in order to assist them with this.

An entrepreneurs that will give up some of the equity in their company can possibly secure quicker funding from an venture capitalists or an angel investor. While this people can give money, something just as valuable can be included such as contacts, advice, and coaching for new entrepreneurs. Crowdfunding, has become a popular tool for young entrepreneurs to raise the funds that they are looking for. An entrepreneur establishes a page for their product with a monetary target to meet. Once this has been accomplished they there are rewards for who gave the money. This can be for actual product to an actual experience.

Bootstrapping for Entrepreneurs.

Bootstrapping is a term used to describe the process of where you start a business entirely using your own money and the proceeds from your first sales. It is challenging because the entrepreneur bears all financial risks and has minimal tolerance for error. By bootstrapping you can run the business according to your vision. Also you have no investor wanting the quick profits from you for their money. But, having support from the outside can sometimes be beneficial rather than harmful. Bootstrapping can by done, but it will be challenging.

Chapter no.3

Characteristics of online Entrepreneurs.

What else do successful business entrepreneurs have in common? For the most part, entrepreneurs are hardworking individuals who delve into areas they are naturally interested in. Passion is undoubtedly the most vital component for startup business owners to have, and every advantage helps. While everyone enjoys the notion of becoming your boss, what with the appeal of making a fortune, the potential setbacks of setting up your own shop are numerous. Income is never guaranteed, employer-sponsored benefits are not always available, and when your company loses money, your personal assets might suffer, not just the company's bottom line. However, by following a few guidelines, you can go a long way toward reducing your risk. A successful internet entrepreneur must possess the following attributes.

1. Versatile.

As you begin your journey, it's crucial to manage all customer interactions, including sales, in the most personal way possible. Direct interaction with customers is the most direct way to get honest feedback on the things your market is most interested in and how you can enhance. If having only one client interface isn't possible, Business owners must train staff to ask for customer feedback as a matter of routine. Customers aren't just encouraged by this, but they're more likely to recommend their businesses to others. One of the most significant advantages that home-based entrepreneurs enjoy over their larger counterparts is the ability to respond to phone calls personally. By just hearing a human voice is a way to entice your new customers and make your existing customers feel appreciated in this time of high-tech backlash. Customers can be frustrated with automated responses and touch-tone menus so by using an personal touch you have already won them over. This is an important fact, given that repeat customers account for roughly 80% of all business. Customers anticipate a very polished website, even though they appreciate more a high-touch telephone service. If you are not in the high-tech sector, online entrepreneurs must still be able to use the Internet to communicate their message to their current and prospective customers. A website that is created by your next door neighbor can be far superior to one created by a $100 million marketing firm. Just verify and feel confident that a live person will answer the phone number listed.

2. Flexible.

Ideas are, however, will evolve. Finding the perfect sweet spot requires trial and error, whether it's a matter of refining the design of a product or altering menu items. The former Starbucks chairman and CEO Howard Schultz first believed that playing Italian opera songs on store speakers would improve an Italian coffeehouse experience that he was trying to recreate. On the other hand, customers had a different view and did not appreciate operas while drinking espresso. In the end, Schultz eliminated the opera and substituted it with comfy chairs.

3. Money Savvy.

The vital ingredient of a profitable new venture is constant cash flow. It is essential for buying items, renting, rent, repairing equipment, and for marketing. The only way to remain financially healthy is to keep accurate financial records of expenses and income. Since most new businesses fail to make a profit within the first year, having cash reserves for contingencies could help entrepreneurs avoid being short of money. Of course, it's essential to make sure that you earn a modest income that will cover the basic needs, but it's not enough. It is particularly true when investing is involved. Of course, making such sacrifices could strain relationships with family members, who could be adjusting to less comfortable living arrangements and fret about their family's assets being ruined. In the end, businesses must discuss the issues and make sure that family members embrace the changes spiritually.

4. Resilient.

Running a business can be extremely difficult, mainly when it's a new venture from the bottom from scratch. It requires a great deal and strong commitment, dedication as well as failure. Successful entrepreneurs will be able to endure regardless of the odds. They have to keep moving forward despite the rejection or failure. Starting an enterprise is a process that has an education curve that isn't easy, mainly when the financial stakes are at stake. If you wish to be successful and be successful, you should never abandon your goals regardless of the odds.

5. Focused.

As a strong person, an excellent leader must stay focused and stay clear of the noise and uncertainties that accompany managing a company. It's a recipe for failure to drift off by your thoughts, doubt your intuitions or ideas, and then get lost in the bigger goal. A successful entrepreneur should not forget why they began their business and remain focused on completing the task.

6. Business Smart.

When you start and run your own business, you must know how to handle the money as well as understand that financial statements. A criticial part of your company is knowing how to understand income, cost and what you can personally do to either increase or decrease them. By making sure you don't run out of money, you will help you keep the firm afloat longer until you can find the proper people for you to manage this. Implementing a sound business strategy that will recognizing your target market, your rivals, as well as your strengths and limitations will help you navigate the challenging environment of running a firm.

7. Communicators.

Effective communication is critical in almost every aspect of both your personal and professional life. Effective communication is also critical in the operation of your business. Successful communication is required for everything in your company from presenting your ideas and strategies to potential investors, to sharing your business plan with your employees, and negotiating contracts with suppliers.

4 Types of Entrepreneurship.

There are several different types of entrepreneurs, and various types of enterprises that they start. The main categories of entrepreneurship are listed below.

Entrepreneurship in Small Businesses.

Small-scale business entrepreneurship refers to the notion of starting a new business without transforming to become a significant company or setting up multiple franchises. Small business entrepreneurship may include a single location eatery, one store, or even a retail store where you sell handmade goods. They usually invest their funds into their venture and prosper if it generates an income and makes a living. They do not have outside investors, and they will only take loans to help maintain the business.

Scalable Startup.

Think of Silicon Valley as an example of a firm that began with a novel concept. The aim is to create an item or service that can help the company grow and scale over time. The firms typically require investors and large amounts of money to develop their business model and expand into new markets.

A large corporation.

A large corporation is the creation of a new business segment within an existing corporation. The present company may be well-positioned to expand into other industries or to become involved in new technology. These companies' CEOs either envision a new market or develop ideas for senior management to begin the process.

Social Entrepreneurship.

The goal of social entrepreneurship is to aid humanity and society in general. The products and services offered are designed to help community members or protect the planet. They are driven by a desire to help the world they live in rather than the desire to make money.

SOCIAL ENTREPRENEUR

The Economy and Entrepreneurs.

According to economists, in a capitalist economy, an entrepreneur serves as a coordinating actor. This coordination manifests itself in the reallocation of resources to new profit opportunities. The entrepreneur moves both essential and intangible resources to promote capital formation. The United States has 32.5 million small companies as of 2021. In a market rife with uncertainty, it is the entrepreneur who makes judgments or takes risks. Entrepreneurs foster efficient discovery and continuously divulge knowledge to the extent that capitalism is a dynamic profit-and-loss system. Established businesses face growing rivalry and challenges from entrepreneurs, which frequently motivates them to invest in R&D. In economic words, the entrepreneur throws a wrench in the system's steady-state equilibrium.

How Entrepreneurship Helps Economies.

In various ways, encouraging entrepreneurship can benefit an economy and society. Entrepreneurs, for starters, launch new firms. They create jobs by inventing goods and services, and they frequently cause a ripple effect that leads to even more significant development. After creating information technology firms in India during the 1990s, companies in related industries like hardware and call center operations providers started to pop up with assistance and products. Entrepreneurs are a significant part of the country's GDP.

Existing enterprises may be restricted to their current markets and eventually reach a revenue ceiling. On the other hand, new items or technology produce new markets and money. Increased employment and incomes can add to a country's tax base, allowing the government to spend more on public initiatives. Entrepreneurs are responsible for bringing about social change. They defy convention with one-of-a-kind creations that minimize reliance on established methods and systems, making them obsolete in some cases. Smartphones and their apps, for example, have changed the way people work and play all around the world. Entrepreneurs promote causes other than their own by investing in community projects and assisting charities and other non-profit organizations. **Bill Gates,** for example, has donated a large portion of his fortune to educational and public-health causes.

Chapter no.4

How to become an online entrepreneur.

The following are the steps to becoming an online entrepreneur:

1. Find a market niche.

Typically, new firms begin by identifying a problem and devising a solution to that problem. Consider what sectors correspond with your knowledge base, skill set, and hobbies if you're thinking about launching an internet business. Finding a business specialization that plays to your strengths will help you stay motivated while also putting your previous skills and expertise to good use.

2. Conduct study

Online business owners should spend time learning about their sector and the tools accessible to them. It may entail researching:

- Social media platforms
- Website development and management
- Digital advertising
- E-commerce software

Speaking with other entrepreneurs about their favorite goods, preferred platforms, triumphs, and obstacles may also be beneficial.

3. **Enroll in classes**

Many schools and universities offer entrepreneurship courses both in-person and online. You can also look for entrepreneur certifications on the Internet. For possible investors, these credentials may lend credibility to your project.

4. **Make a business strategy**

Many online entrepreneurs must communicate their idea to a variety of people, including:

- Other business owners
- Friends and family
- Financial advisors.
- Investors

A good business plan organizes and professionalizes your research, plans, and objectives so that readers can learn more about your long-term ambitions. The sections of a business strategy are as follows:

- Executive summary
- Company description

- Market analysis
- Competitive analysis
- Organizational structure
- Description of products or services
- Marketing plan
- Sales strategy
- Funding request
- Financial projections.

5. Network.

Being connected to other experts in your field and the digital business world will allow you to spread your business to the appropriate people. It is also possible to connect with potential strategic partners and service providers for your company. You can network by;

- Engaging with companies or individuals on social media
- Attending professional events, such as conferences and workshops
- Joining professional and recreational groups.

6. Advertise your business.

Create an advertising campaign to notify potential customers and clients about your firm once you're ready to launch it. You might think about using the following tools:

- Digital ads
- Social media ads
- Email campaigns.

Make sure to target your adverts to your designated market to get the most out of your marketing investment. For example, if you are running an online boutique shop that only accepts orders for pick-up, your adverts should target customers in your neighborhood.

Online entrepreneur skills.

Successful online entrepreneurs often have the following skills:

Digital marketing skills.

A solid personal brand, which you can create through digital marketing, is essential for online entrepreneurship. Because most entrepreneurs work on a shoestring budget, it's critical to leverage digital marketing skills to raise brand awareness and produce leads on a budget. Determine your company's unique selling points compared to its competitors and concentrate your marketing efforts on them. When starting an online business, consistency is crucial. You should publish frequently and interact with your fans and other brands on social media. The following are examples of digital marketing:

- Websites
- Blogs
- Digital video channels
- Emails.

Search engine optimization.

Search engine Optimization (SEO) refers to an expression that describes strategies that aid your website to get higher rankings within search result pages. SEO can increase the number of people who visit your site, increasing brand awareness and revenues.

- Using popular keywords in your content
- Regularly updating your content
- Creating optimized metadata and other back-end descriptions
- Analyzing user trends and altering methods are some of the components of SEO.

Copywriting and content creation.

Being proficient in copywriting and content production can help you save money, improve productivity, and advertise your products or services because you may be able to fulfill many of your business' functions with a small crew. Regular updates to your website's content, social media feeds, and video channels can help you enhance your search rankings and boost customer engagement.

Time management.

Online entrepreneurs must manage their time correctly because they work on a short budget and small team.

- Organization: Business owners must devise ways to keep track of their obligations, essential dates, and project status.
- Prioritization: Entrepreneurs must decide which tasks are the most critical and require immediate attention.

- Delegation: Successful business owners hire individuals they can trust and assign everyday responsibilities to them, giving them more time to concentrate on higher-level organizational planning.

Salary and job outlook for online entrepreneurs.

According to Indeed salaries, entrepreneurs in the United States earn an average of $46,453 a year. Profit-sharing pays them an extra $6,500 per year on average. While data on internet entrepreneurs isn't accessible, the US Bureau of Labor Statistics estimates 9.6 million self-employed people in the United States in 2016. According to the BLS, self-employed professionals will rise to 10.3 million by 2026, representing a 7.9% increase.

Chapter no.5

Successful Online Entrepreneur.

Entrepreneurs from the America United States earn an average of $46,453 per year, according to salaries from Indeed. Profit-sharing gives entrepreneurs an additional $6,500 per year, on average. Although data on online entrepreneurs aren't available, a US Bureau of Labour Statistics estimates 9.6 million self-employed workers within the United States in 2016. Based on the BLS estimates, the number of self-employed workers will increase to 10.3 million by 2026. It is an increase of 7.9 percent growth. Anyone could begin their business journey, but it's difficult to imagine taking a risk and leaving the security of a full-time position with healthcare insurance and a wage to start a business on your own. I can relate to this since I had similar worries when I started my own company. Today I'd like to show you what you should learn about online business and guide you through the steps to begin and be successful as you are your boss.

- **Understand You're "Why"**

Before you embark on your online business journey, it is essential to know why you want to start your own company at all.

- Are you seeking freedom?
- A passive income lifestyle?
- Potential for earning.
- To make all the choices and be your boss?
- Do you find yourself hating your job?
- Are you looking to get involved with something you're interested in?

No matter what you're using to work full-time, there needs to be a rationale or a list of motives. It was for me because of freedom and the potential to earn. Find out what is essential for you, and this will enable you to be successful even when the going gets tough.

- **Don't Leave Your Full-Time Job…yet.**

I'm not a massive lover of quitting your job full-time and placing all your bets on the possibility of starting a small-scale business on your own. The reason for this is quite simple. Whether or not you're a business online, 45% of small-scale enterprises have a failure in the initial five years.

I'm a big fan of taking calculated risk-taking. Given that many entrepreneurs fail, I believe it's more rational to work full-time as you start and end with a side hustle. It will help you make better decisions as your finances will not be stressed. If people are concerned about their finances and make it the main objective of their business instead of what their clients want, they're from being able to run a successful online business.

2. Business Idea That Fits Your Lifestyle.

An appealing aspect of an online business, also called virtual real estate, could provide impressive passive income potential. It is probably one of the top motives to start. But my many experiences have taught me the "passive income" model isn't the ideal choice for everyone? What's the reason? It can take a lot of time to earn enough money to cover your work, as I've demonstrated in my article on income. It is essential to know that having a business idea attractive to others doesn't necessarily have to be the best for you. Pick a theme that's an expression of the way you'd like your life to look.

Here's an overview of some concepts to think about:

Create a blog: I consider this my favorite business model since it's incredibly inactive once you've figured out how it functions. The majority of this model relies on advertising on display and affiliate marketing to generate revenue. Although it's beneficial to know about the basics of SEO and the digital market, it's not required.

Becoming a YouTuber: My second-favorite business model, mainly because of how easy it is. Although most people believe that YouTube needs you to be in front of a camera and complete a 60-hour working week to be successful, it's not the case when you approach the process differently. I refer to it as a "themed channel." It means you'll begin making cash online, mainly with YouTube AdSense income.

Make yourself an online consultant. There are many kinds of consulting jobs that you could begin helping other small companies. You could be a social media manager, general marketer or Search Engine Optimization (SEO) specialist and web design specialist (assuming you are familiar with the software for web design), a programmer, or whatever else fits your abilities. While this isn't the ideal way to become an internet-based entrepreneur, since it's not a passive endeavor, it's an excellent way to get started if this is your first experience.

Start an online business: There are many different platforms to buy and sell products or develop and market products by starting from scratch. It isn't a passive endeavor and usually requires some money to start, but it can be very profitable when you've made it to the top. There are a variety of platforms that you can use to start your own business; I'd suggest you study my article on selling on retail or selling on Etsy to begin.

Teach other people skills: Hundreds, perhaps thousands, of entrepreneurs online who sell online courses to earn an income. Although it requires enormous effort to develop the concept of a course and outline, it's an excellent method to become an online business owner who succeeds since you can draw on your previous experience and expertise to make it work. You'll need to locate the most appropriate internet-based platform for courses to run your business. Then, you'll create and market your course. If your courses achieve been successful, you could consider the possibility of private labeling and the PLR course to generate an alternative income stream.

- **Learn While You Go**

If you're trying to figure out the best way to become an online business owner, you must realize how the "just-in-time" method of learning can assist you in your success. In the same way, information overload is the norm in this field. To counter this, start your company first, and then concentrate on learning all you have to be aware of. When you try to grasp *the basics* before you begin, likely, you won't ever start. Let's say, for instance, you'd like to be a blogger, based on my recommendations. That's GREAT! However, if you aren't sure how to utilize WordPress or are only beginning in online marketing, it could prevent you from even beginning because of feeling overwhelmed.

- **Get Started Now.**

One of the most common issues entrepreneurs who consider starting their own business is spending their time fretting about the best business model and creating an effective business plan. If you are determined to become an online business owner, the first step you have to do is establish yourself. I can say that the number one regret for those who have been accomplished in their fields for me, too, is not having started earlier. I'm not sure why people do not start. However, most people are afraid to fail and conclude that the best way to proceed is not to begin. Started...therefore, they are unable to fail. You're going to fail, and it's OK; I grant you the right to fail. I've failed several times myself. Although it sounds like a cliché, it's almost a rite of passage to begin something and then fall flat on their face. The "failure" is learning about what works and what doesn't. It's a constant failure when you fail and then give up. The most practical advice I can give yours. Don't give up.

- **Create a Plan and stick to It.**

Before you begin your online venture, it is essential to establish a plan for yourself and adhere to it strictly. It is particularly essential for those with children or starting an online business as an additional side hustle. How many hours do you work? What days will you be working less? How will you handle your workload with your current obligations? I would suggest an hour or less every workday during the week, and a minimum of 3-4 hours on weekends. The key is to be consistent. If you're able in your online venture, even just an hour every day, the hours add up and result in an excellent end-product.

- **Do your best to work hard.**

Work. Concentrate on becoming highly efficient and then work hard by putting your head to the max. Keep in mind that someone is trying to beat you every moment you're not working. Remember, your online business is how you escape your current position. It doesn't matter if you're employed at a job you love, but you dislike, or in a jobless state and would like to create your own company from scratch. Working hard is the solution to your problems.

- **Don't be afraid to experiment with the new stuff.**

One of the things I discovered when I became an online entrepreneur was trying new ideas to boost your income and find out the most successful things. I've developed classes online on Udemy and my website and built various blogs/websites. I've also attempted to sell online, delved into affiliate marketing, and tried different other things to increase my earnings. **Most of** them have been faced failures; however, a handful of them was successful, and it takes only a few to sustain your career as an online businessman.

- **Make Short-Term Goals.**

Many people spend the majority of their time composing goals. I think it's a bit absurd because you don't know what will transpire in the next year. The present. Me? I would suggest setting goals for the month, and that's it. Grab a sheet of paper or purchase a whiteboard from Amazon and consider the things you could be able to get completed by the end of the month. Write it down. After you're finished, place that whiteboard or piece of paper in the place where you're working every day so that you can constantly remind yourself and press yourself to reach them. That's it. Set/achieve your targets. If you can do this each month for a year, you'll have made tons of progress and will begin making cash online.

- **Don't be afraid to decide to invest.**

What do you think the chances of success for Amazon could be If Jeff Bezos never invested anything into the company? What do you think of Google? What about Facebook? These companies needed capital investment to succeed; the founders believed in the vision enough to take risks with their capital. Remember that your company will need some money and therefore don't be afraid to invest within your budget. My suggestion is to develop an initial budget that you are comfortable with everyone month.

- **Reinvest Profits from Your Business.**

If you do finally start earning money, you must reinvest every penny. **Do not** take payment for at least six months. If you can do this successfully and efficiently, you will grow your business by leaps and bounds. I've seen this firsthand. It's tough to become massive if you are spending most of your time blogging and filming videos, addressing customer complaints (considering having a virtual phone number to deal with this), or anything else you're able to outsource.

Be comfortable with outsourcing when you're profitable and willing to invest in the product you've built. It will enable you to focus on the more significant issues and the direction for your business. I hope this article can help you realize the challenges of being an owner of an online business. These tips have been learned through experience, and I hope they will aid you along your journey.

Chapter no.6

Become an entrepreneur without money and experience.

You are your boss making all the decisions working hard to reach your goals -- for a lot of individuals, entrepreneurship is the ultimate goal for a career. However, as unique as having your own business may sound. However, it's tough. How hard is it? Ninety percent of **startups fail**. Entrepreneurs are **more stressed than the rest of us** and suffer from more everyday stress. When you're accountable for your bottom line, every failure falls upon you. The good thing is that starting a business can be among the most rewarding, thrilling, exciting chances you'll ever have if you're aware of the dangers and are still determined to become an entrepreneur, the tips and strategies from this guide.

How to Become an entrepreneur.

- Find profitable startup concepts.
- Focus on and identify the fastest-growing categories (or groups).
- To meet an unmet demand.
- Create something superior (or less expensive) than the current offerings.
- Check your startup's concept with the research of your buyer.
- Begin with a minimum-viable production (MVP).

- Make a business plan.
- Keep iterating Based on feedback.
- Find an associate founder.

1. Find profitable startup concepts.

The foundation of a successful business is an idea. It's impossible to build a successful company without an idea. Here are some innovative strategies for thinking about an idea for a product or service. **Find out what is bothering them.** What makes a service successful? It solves an issue or frustration that people will spend money to alleviate. In this way, begin by asking your friends what frustrates them. Entrepreneurs find inspiration in their everyday frustrations. For example:

- Travis Kalanick and Garret Camp **began Uber** following a time when they struggled to find a taxi.
- Chris Riccobono **created UNTUCK it** Chris Riccobono launched Untucking assortment of shirts with a good look without tucking them

in after becoming annoyed by how wrinkled and un-shape his button-down shirts appeared when he didn't tie them into.

While you think about your ideas and brainstorm, have your group of friends keep track of the daily items that make them angry. Go through their lists and search for any issues you might be able to resolve.

Learn from other startups in the making.

Looking at what others have created can be an excellent method to kick your thinking process into high gear. Check out **the product Hunt**, an ongoing collection of the latest apps, websites, games, and websites for inspiration in the digital world. In addition, **Kickstarter** is an excellent resource for physical items. There are plenty of review sites for products that can spark your imagination.

Look for trends to help you futureproof your concept.

As the world evolves and people require different products. In this case, the rise of Uber, Lyft, and other ride-sharing applications resulted in a need for a third-party application that can inform you of the most affordable fares available at that time. Check out trends predictions for your industry or market or look up general trend forecasting publications such as **Trend Hunter** and **Spring wise**. Ask yourself, "If these predictions are accurate, what tools will be required?"

2. Choose and concentrate on the fastest-growing categories (or the categories).

Expert in-licensing and strategist for intellectual property **Stephen Key recommends** choosing a field that entices you but doesn't become too competitive. "I prefer to stay away from areas that are notoriously difficult such as the toy business. There are a lot of people working in that field," he explains."You will have a much easier to license your ideas if you concentrate on the categories of products which are expanding and are open to innovation that is open." Once you've selected the category you want to study, the key says you should examine all the products within that category.

- What are the advantages of each product, as well as how do they differ?
- What is their marketing and packaging strategy?
- What do reviewers think?
- What improvements could be made?

After picking a product, consider questions like:

- What can we do to enhance it?
- Can I add a new feature?
- What do you think about a different type of material?
- Can I personalize it?

3. To meet an unmet demand.

Many entrepreneurs start successful businesses when they spot an opportunity. For instance, you might discover that there is a lack of top-quality outsourcing of sales. As you've had experience in sales development and account management in early-stage sales firms, it is possible to provide this service to startups in the tech industry.

4. Create something superior (or less expensive) than what's available.

It's not always to come up with something new. If you can offer an existing product for sale at a lower cost or with higher quality, or, ideally, both, you'll get plenty of potential customers. In addition, there's an ongoing demand. While you are going through your day, you should make an inventory of the things you do. Review the list to find anything you could change.

Other ideas

- **Connect with fellow entrepreneurs.** Utilize Eventbrite or Meetup to search for events within the area's startup communities. Not only will connecting with other entrepreneurs help you establish beneficial relationships, but it'll provide you with plenty of concepts.
- **Patent applications for research:** Patent applications are generally made public around about 18 months after they have been filed. While we do not advise outright

copying inventions, a glance through these documents will provide a sense of where the field is heading.

- **Brainstorming session:** To get your creative juices flowing, invite three to five other entrepreneurial-minded people to a brainstorming session. Invite everyone to talk about a specific topic or issue, for example, "What's your favorite type of X and why?" Or "Do you have any tools to achieve what you want to accomplish? Do you have a reason why or not?" The answers could result in some beautiful ideas.

5. Check your startup's concept with customer persona research.

It's great, you've thought of something. But don't quit your day job yet. Before you get all in, you must be aware of the people who will want your product. (No family members, friends, or relatives don't cut.) able to assess the effectiveness of your product on the marketplace, begin by **knowing your buyer's persona**, i.e., the people to who you want to sell your product. If your product isn't addressing an actual need, they'll never be interested in it, no matter how cool or innovative it may be. That's why buyer personas and market research is so crucial. After you've found your ideal customer, interviewing those who match the criteria is an essential part of your investigation. Give them a live demonstration of your service, then ask them whether they are satisfied and dislike and how much they'd spend for it and how often they'd utilize it, and so on.

If you're looking to gauge customers' interest before launching any other product, create your landing page to explain the product or service you offer. Request that people submit their email addresses for an early access period, an unpaid subscription, membership or product, a discount, new product announcements, or other attractive deals. Promote the video via social, paid search, and so on. And see the number of visitors who convert into registrations.

6. Begin with a minimum-viable production (MVP).

The MVP version is the most basic and straightforward version you can make of the product or service you could offer. It's sufficient to please the first customers and get an idea of how you can improve. Let's say you're looking to create an app that connects students to tutors via virtual. You could create a minimal version, invite manually 150 tutors from the Internet to sign up, and publish the link to the application on the campus's Facebook page. If you're able to get a decent number of people signing up, it's an indication that you need to take the next step. If you receive a few signs, you may want to reconsider the concept or make a fresh start. Start small, and using an MVP reduces costs while allowing space for growth as your product is verified.

7. Develop a business strategy.

The business plan can be described as a formal document that outlines your business objectives and the steps to reach these goals. It could include a marketing strategy and budget as well as financial projections as well as milestones. In your role as an entrepreneur, the task is to establish your company's goals, mission, and short-term and long-term goals. While you are doing this kind of plan for the strategic development of your business, the business plan is the result of your efforts and aids in your company's growth.

8. Keep iterating in response to feedback.

Be aware that your MVP may not likely be sufficient to stay relevant in the markets you select, particularly when you have big goals for your company. The next step is creating enthusiasm and prospects (marketing products), securing customers (selling your product), gauging satisfaction, and improving the product based on the feedback... And then repeat. The ability to optimize all the components of this flywheel can generate the income required to invest in the product, and investment in the product will generate additional interest from:

- Customers who are satisfied with their service create word-of-mouth referrals
- More competitive options that attract new customers.

9. Find an investor who is a co-founder

It is a common belief that you should seek out the co-founder of your own business. There are three advantages to having a co-founder.

1. It's much easier to raise funds. It doesn't matter if having several founders contribute to the success of a business; however, many venture capitalists believe that it is. They're not inclined to invest in sole founders.

2. You're supported emotionally. The running of a business is an arduous, thrilling, and challenging experience. If you're on the emotional rollercoaster all on your own, you don't have anyone to share your joy with when things go well -- or get through the downs. A co-founder knows what you're experiencing and helps you feel less isolated.

3. They could offer different skills or knowledge and connections. Perhaps you're good in

sales, whereas your co-founder has more technical skills. There are many connections and have launched an enterprise before. The choice of a co-founder with personal resumes is a fantastic method to increase your chances of success.

However, there are disadvantages to having co-founders.

1. There will be conflicts. You and your partner will always be at odds. A healthy debate can be productive; however, you'll be wasting valuable effort and time if you fail to arrive at a resolution quickly. In addition, you could harm the morale of your team.

2. There's a need to divide all equity. If you are the sole owner of your business and you're the sole owner, you'll start with 100 percent equity. When time passes, and you add more employees or receive funds, you'll divide this equity. However, you'll likely give 0.005 percentage up to 35% of the equity to one entity, based on the person they're. If you're co-founders, you'll automatically give up 40 to 60% of your company in one go.

3. Finding one isn't easy. It isn't easy to find someone who has similar business ethics or work style and a similar personality. Furthermore, they have to be convinced of your vision and have the appropriate capabilities, and also have the desire to become your co-founders in the first place. It's not an easy task. It's important to note that there are many examples of successful companies with one founder, as in the same way, unsuccessful startups

failed due to conflicts between co-founders. Choose a course of action in the light of your circumstance and not on conventional advice.

How to find a Founder or Co-Founder.

If you've decided to co-found a company, your next task is to find one. Consider your network first. You can choose someone you know or whose acquaintances can confirm is safer than selecting an unknown person. It is a reverse-engineering strategy, and you've had a greater chance of getting them to join your group when they're in a first- and second-degree relationship. However, if you've reached out to your networks but haven't had any luck, There are several "co-founder connecting" services that you can use.

- **Stealth. li**
- **the Founder Nation**

You may also go to local entrepreneurial events to connect with potential partners.

How to Get Funding.

It is necessary to invest cash to make money. To finance your startup, you can consider these alternatives:

1. Your family and friends should be encouraged to contribute to your business.

Many entrepreneurs rely on family and friends for an initial investment. It is typically known as "seed round. "Seed round." You can trade funds for an investment in your startup (i.e., that your relative gets 4 percent of the company after you give them $12,000). You can also ask for a private loan (with or without interest) or even make donations.

2. Request a small-business grant.

State, federal, and local governments offer programs for small companies, such as loan programs with low rates of interest and venture capital and grants. Many businesses aren't eligible for the program, and therefore, you may not be able to locate any. However, it's worth investigating since it's free money!

3. Use a crowdfunding platform.

Kickstarter, Indiegogo, GoFundMe, Fundable, and many other crowdfunding platforms allow you to get funding via campaigns online. This approach doesn't just help you create capital, but it also enables you to gain early feedback on your product and brand recognition. And often, if you've got an exciting story to tell or a fantastic product, then press.

4. Present your pitch to an angel investor.

Angel investors look for early-stage companies which can double or even triple their investment. They typically invest between $25,000 and $50,000. In this regard, they'll consider the potential value of a company's future and how easy it'll be to achieve it. They'll be meticulous in ensuring that you're aware of your client's requirements and the market within which you operate and also the ways you'll earn money and how you'll increase it. You must be prepared with solid business plans and initial signs of success (such as "the typical user refers two additional users within their very first week" or "we increased our revenue by a third between January and the month of March.") In addition to angel's funds; you'll have access to their experience and connections. In exchange, they'll be able to exchange equity.

5. Venture capital solicitation.

Venture capitalists are looking for small, private businesses that are young and growing. Like angel investors, VC firms seek high-risk investment opportunities that yield high returns. The return they are looking for is contingent on how mature your company is. If they invest before the company goes public or is purchased, a 3X return is good. However, if a VC firm invests early, it's likely to be seeking a 7X to 10X return.

6. Utilize a credit card to get the short-term cash option.

It's generally not recommended to utilize your credit card for business expenses unless, of course, you have the funds to pay the remaining balance. Sometimes, there's no other choice but to pay cash, and it's urgent. But losing your credit score and piling an excessive amount of credit card debt could affect your business over the long term (not to mention your financial wellbeing).

7. You can get a microloan.

You can't take out a loan during the first year of your business since lenders aren't ready to make such a risky investment. But you can avail the microloan program offered by the Small Business Administration program. Small-scale businesses can be granted up to $50,000, while the average SBA loan is $13,000. Microlenders and non-profit lenders are two other choices. They usually target minority or marginalized entrepreneurs. The terms of their loans are generally fair. NerdWallet's guide for the best non-profit lending institutions across the US is an excellent source.

8. Bootstrap it.

There is no need to take any money from anybody other than you wish to. Some businesses don't even raise money in the first place. Their founders cover their initial expenses on their own; then, once the business is profitable, the revenue it earns covers the entire cost. This option lets you (and your co-founders) keep more of your business if you already have one. But your company may not grow as quickly and without significant funding. If you decide to start a business from scratch, ensure that you make sure your budget is as slim as you can to extend the life of your business.

How to incorporate your business.

At some time, you will need to decide if you would like to incorporate your company. As a sole proprietor, both your company and you will be considered one entity. When you incorporate your business, it becomes distinct from you. From a legal point of view, it can purchase and sell properties, pay taxes, sue and be sued, create contracts, and commit other crimes.

The Benefits of incorporating.

Most importantly, a company protects its assets from the burden of business obligations and debts. Creditors typically seek to pay from the company's assets but not your assets (like your home, car, or bank account, and other such things). Also, you're not legally accountable for the company's actions. Anyone who sues your company will be suing your company. The corporation you are in allows you to transfer shares. You can also sell a part of your stake in an organization, transfer it to another company, or even give it away. If you are looking to accept external investment or bring an additional partner, it is necessary to sell. The status of a corporation also provides you with more credibility, which can help you get investment capital. In addition, businesses can deduct business expenses before allocating the income.

The disadvantages of incorporating.

It adds a tax burden. You'll have to regularly file your tax returns with the state and pay annual fees. The process is long and time-consuming. Hiring an attorney can range between a few hundred and thousands of dollars. There's no need to incorporate because there are various corporate structures that you can pick from. However, it's a great idea to incorporate if you have a co-founder, require external funds, or want legal protection. After you've chosen to incorporate, you'll need to select between becoming a limited liability corporation (LLC) or an S corporation. The SBA provides a helpful guide for picking the best organizational structure.

Entrepreneur Help & Support.
Financial Resources.

As we mentioned earlier, entrepreneurs generally expand their business through bootstrapping (securing the funds themselves) by utilizing micro-business loans or getting investors' funding. Here are some resources you can look at:

- **SBA Financial Programs** The SBA aids find financiers, secure investment capital, secure grants, and more.
- **Incubators** for startups offer resources to expand the business by granting equity. A lot of incubators are dependent on the location or industry. However, organizations like the International Business Innovation Association and Incubator List can help connect you to incubators.

- **Angel investing.** Angel Investor uses their funds to invest and focus on helping entrepreneurs develop and expand in exchange for equity. Many angel investing communities are also location-dependent; however, organizations like Seed Invest and AngelList can assist you in pitching for accredited investors.
- **Venture Capital** - Venture capitalists do not invest with their own money. They invest, so they are taking fewer risks and are less willing to agree on conditions, which is the reason you should steer clear of VC financing until you're established in your company. Gust and the National Venture Capital Association and Gust can assist you in raising VC capital.

Advocacy and Counseling.

The gap in finances isn't the only hurdle to overcome in entrepreneurship. You might also face the issue of knowledge gaps. It is where counseling, training, and advocacy are crucial.

- SBA Learning Center. The SBA provides a learning platform "designed to educate and empower small business owners of the process." This includes courses, business guides, and programs for development.
- **Business Hubs**. Local governments may create businesses that combine affordable workspace, networks, and other resources that help small businesses create a local economy. They are entirely local-specific and are more prevalent in cities, but make sure you research the possibility of an initiative in your local area.
- **Professional and Trade Associations and Business Groups. Membership in a professional organization could help you build confidence with your customers; however, it usually comes with extra benefits, such as job boards, legal resources, courses for training,g, and much more**. These are usually location- or specific to the industry.

Support Networks.

When you decide to pursue business ownership, you could face an uphill climb about specific aspects of ownership of a business and management. One aspect of being aware is that you do not need to face the challenges and tribulations yourself. This learning process can be slowed and reduced through participation in entrepreneurial networks, groups, and events to gain knowledge. Your problem or area of weakness could be one that a group member has encountered before, and you could benefit from their experience. Additionally, you could have information that could assist other entrepreneurs who are in need. Here's how to go about developing your support network

- **Find and participate in events for entrepreneurs**. The SBA provides both in-person and online activities for entrepreneurs. Use the search function to find events that are most appropriate for your specific situation.
- **Join existing organizations and peer advisory panels** organizations like the Entrepreneurs Organization and The Tugboat Institute, and Vistage provides membership and support for entrepreneurs.
- **You can find an expert business coach or mentor.** A personal approach from a coach or mentor can assist you in tackling issues in a one-on-one manner and assist you in growing as a leader.

The path to becoming an entrepreneur isn't easy, but it's incredibly satisfying.

Chapter no.7

Drawbacks & Benefits of Online Business.

What is Online Business?

The definition of online business is the business activities that take place via the Internet. When a company creates an online store to sell its products, customers purchase their goods through the Internet.

In which countries is Online Business used?

The rise of technology on the Internet has transformed the way businesses run their business—numerous industries such as cinema, transportation as well as medical use websites to communicate to their customers. Many companies rely entirely on the Internet. Even though an online company operates like a traditional company but there are some distinct advantages and disadvantages. The advantages and disadvantages are significant to consider before starting an online business.

Benefits from Online Business Credibility.

One advantage of this company model is the fact that it gives credibility. To begin using a brick-and-mortar model, you'll typically have to put up a lot of money into infrastructure. Customers and other businesses are aware of this, and this demonstrates your dedication to the marketplace. Anyone can begin with an online business for just a couple hundred dollars. A brick-and-mortar-based business shows that you're looking for the long-term.

Selling perishables.

Having a brick-and-mortar store is beneficial if you have a company that sells perishable food items, such as an upscale grocery store. Although some businesses offer food on the Internet, having a physical shop that customers can go to will give you an edge in this marketplace. The process of fresh shipping food can be complex and frequently leads to damage or spoilage. If you have a brick-and-mortar place, this lets you get food items and then sell them promptly to ensure that they are fresh when delivered to the consumer.

Different Payment Methods.

A brick-and-mortar store permits you to accept various payment options from your customers. If you can increase the variety of available payment methods, it improves the likelihood of completing the sale. For instance, if, for example, you run an online store generally, you can accept payments via debit or credit card or an external payment processor such as PayPal. If you are operating a brick-and-mortar establishment, you can accept checks and cash too.

Costs for the long term.

Businesses that operate online have significantly lower operating costs than traditional businesses. An online business requires very little office space or no need to have an office even. Thus, companies can cut down on the expense of leasing physical offices. Additionally, if there's no physical location for business, eventually, the cost of hiring employees will be decreased.

Customization.

The degree of satisfaction provided by an online company is higher than that of an office-based traditional business. An unrivaled business model offers a greater degree of customization in online business. In an online store, there are many options for customization available to the customer. Customers must choose one option and place the purchase. Using these steps, it is possible to enhance the customer's experience.

The availability.

A business that is run online is not subject to limitations on time, as opposed to traditional businesses that are subject to opening and closing hours. Online stores are open 24/7; they offer more significant opportunities to make sales. Based on their needs, customers can make purchases at any time if they have internet access.

Accessibility.

Online companies are also free of geographical limitations. Customers can make an order from anywhere on the globe. But only if you have access to the Internet. It is among the reasons businesses prefer online strategies to reach international clients.

The Adaptation.

If you are the owner of your own online company, you are entitled to the authority to adjust the market requirements. If it's a personal blog or an online store, the user is granted the right to update. In the event of an update being made, the user will be informed immediately via email marketing or any other method of communication.

6. Customer Data.

A crucial aspect of every business is collecting information about customers. Online companies allow customers to collect data about their customers and their behavior. It's all done with minimum effort. The company can make the necessary changes to improve customer experience by analyzing these data. For instance, for an online store, it is possible to determine the most exciting products, the country from which the most significant sales originate, and the most popular payment method.

7. Customer Contact.

Through an online company, you can connect with customers from all over the world. Anyone visiting from any specific region is more likely to be a potential customer for your business. Even small businesses have an opportunity to connect with customers from all over the world. In the end, this could lead to the highest sales that cannot be effectively achieved through offline business.

The disadvantages of online Business.
1. Cost of starting.

While online businesses can benefit from cost savings over time, it's not the same regarding implementation. The business has to be prepared to deal with the enormous initial cost as the website needs to be created and maintained by professionals.

Furthermore, there are additional costs related to SEO and hosting, which could increase overall costs.

2. Security.

Many people aren't at ease with the idea of conducting transactions through the Internet for business. The rapid growth of online transactions has attracted the attention of hackers. There have been numerous fraud cases where fake businesses use financial information to scam customers. Because of this, consumers are hesitant to share private information online.

3. Competition.

Running an online business isn't an easy task because of the fierce competition with the online world. The big corporations always come with more effective promotions, marketing, and lower-priced products that can remove your business from you. If the right business strategy is not followed, the company could be facing significant loss.

4. Trust.

Online business is an entirely online process. It is not based on any human interaction. The process of gaining trust from customers is not easy to achieve in this case. Particularly for small businesses with no reliable brand name. It may take time to establish they are genuine.

5. Customer Satisfaction.

It is evident that in online businesses such as e-commerce websites, customers aren't allowed to interact with the product physically. However, when the product is given to the customer, there is no guarantee that they'll be pleased with the product. If the purchaser does not get the desired product, they may return the product.

6. Technical Issues.

It is common for websites to experience downtime. In the same way, if your business website encounters issues, customers could be presented with an error notification. If the error isn't corrected, the problem will persist for several days. It could stop customers from conducting business transactions or even visiting your website.

7. Customer Support.

In contrast to a traditional business, an internet-based company cannot have face-to-face interactions. It is a significant issue for customers as the majority of them prefer direct communications.

Although some businesses online provide contact via chat, email, or contact customer service, it's not enough to provide the quality of service that comes from a face-to-face conversation.

Differences Between E-Business and Traditional Business.

Entrepreneurs planning to launch the business of their dreams must consider the differentiators between an online business and an established business model. The differences don't mean that one is superior to the other. One model might be more used for specific kinds of business services and products. Certain businesses can benefit from a mix of both models.

The difference with regards to Overhead costs.

Most E-business models are less expensive in terms of overhead and startup costs than traditional models of business that use brick-and-mortar stores. Removing the need for place costs, staff, and the utilities required for brick-and-mortar stores helps companies boost their profits. If you choose to go with a brick-and-mortar model will also require an online presence. Costs for development and marketing aren't eliminated from the traditional business model. Many of the latest e-commerce models use affiliate marketing with big companies like Amazon or drop-shipping companies like Shopify. It reduces the cost of operations by removing the requirement for inventory entirely.

Importance of Convenience for Consumers.

The rise of online business has made it increasingly difficult for traditional retailers to compete with shoppers looking for an easy shopping experience. But there's an audience of customers who prefer an actual shopping experience and the chance to look at the products and try on clothes. Some consumers also appreciate the personal interactions offered by brick-and-mortar stores. A few businesses can be adapted to a strict e-business model. Doctors, lawyers, and dentists aren't able to provide their services exclusively online.

Different Marketing Strategies.

Businesses that solely operate online typically have a bigger budget for marketing on the Internet than traditional businesses. Traditional companies typically diversify their marketing strategies to draw customers from local areas and the online population. Businesses that sell online invest more time in blogs, social media, and advertisements for search engines. Facebook pages are now one of the most increasingly popular methods of e-business marketing and brand recognition. Some online businesses depend solely on budget-friendly or no-budget campaign marketing, whereas others run advertisements that have large budgets. Traditional businesses typically use the same methods on the Internet, but occasionally to a lesser degree. Brick and mortar shops may require printed ads, mailers, or other niche ads like advertisements on bus benches or wagons for grocery stores. Commercials on television and radio in local markets are another way traditional businesses can reach new customers.

Tempo and accessibility.

Online stores are always available, and shoppers can complete transactions in just a few minutes. The journey to and from traditional businesses shopping, looking over the merchandise, speaking with salespeople, and even waiting in several lines to make a purchase consume valuable time. E-commerce companies can sell goods and services all week, all day long. Week. A few traditional businesses are not accessible 24 hours a day, but certain ones are. Many brick-and-mortar establishments close on weekends, and some are open just 5 or 6 days, seven days.

Chapter no.8

Understand Operating an Online Business.

Beginning a lingerie business online can have some similarities to running a brick-and-mortar store; however, there are many considerations that an online retailer must consider to be successful in the world of e-commerce. Although you won't need to pay for rent or utility bills or have to worry about cleaning or maintaining your shop when you're an online-only retailer, you will need to take into consideration issues like:

- Hosting costs for websites.
- Cybersecurity
- Choose the suitable platform for your store
- Conducting effective digital marketing.

The margin of profit for online lingerie sales is likely to differ from the profit margin for the retail lingerie market due to the cost savings associated with an online company. Your products should be priced according to the prices you see for similar items in other stores online. Pricing them that they would be sold in physical shops will result in lower sales and consequently lower profits for you. If you're selling online lingerie as a separate segment of your lingerie business instead of a new business, you should price your products similarly both online and in-store. Price differences can be confusing and cause a stir among buyers. The process of marketing an online business is distinct from the marketing of bricks-and-mortar shops. If you operate an online business, the majority or nearly all of your marketing activities are done electronically, for example, through social media, content marketing advertisements, as well as your mailing list. Being aware of SEO concepts and effective digital marketing strategies is essential for any online business.

Create a Clear Business Vision.

Before you write an outline of your business, develop an elaborate vision of your company. Ask yourself these questions, as well as any follow-up questions that naturally arise from your answers:

- Am I planning to launch my lingerie line or sell products from other designers?

- Is this a solely online business, or will physical retail establishments, such as an actual store, a chain of shops, or even pop-up shops?

- What is my initial budget?

- Who is my ideal client?

- What are my ideal buyers currently offered by the online market for lingerie?

- Where can I get my items?

In the business planning process, Begin to brainstorm names for your company. After that, go on the Internet to see if there are any existing online lingerie stores -- or any other type of business that have the same names you're contemplating. You can't start a business in your state using a name that a registered company in the state is already using.

Create the Business Plan.

One of the important actions to begin a lingerie company is to write an effective business plan. The business plans a detailed document that provides everything for the business partner, owner, or prospective buyer to know about the business, for example:

- The place where the company is headquartered
- The day-to-day operations of the business.
- What will the business startup be supported?
- The team that runs the company's management
- The way the company is formed
- The company's debts and anticipated expenses
- The projected profits of the business
- What are the products and services that the company offers?
- Information on the market for which you are targeting.

Incorporate the company through your state's Internal Revenue Service (IRS) and also with your state. Though you might be able to run a company without registering it through your state, the IRS, and your local government if you run the business as a sole proprietor, it's generally in your best interest to register your business legally segregate you from. If a business is not registered and is not registered, the company **and the business owner** are legally the same entity.

Create The Store You Want to Create Online Store.

The next step to start an online business selling lingerie is to determine exactly what and where you'll sell your products online. **This choice will**

affect the profitability margin. The options for online retailers are:

- Setting up a store on a reputable online retailer, like Amazon or Etsy
- The creation of an online store is done through an online platform such as Shopify
- Designing an e-commerce site from the ground up.

Setting up a seller account on platforms like Amazon, eBay or Etsy is the most convenient method to start an online shop selling lingerie. Using this method, you do not have any technical responsibility, and you can list your products and sell them via the platform. The disadvantages of this method are the charges imposed by the platform and the inability to customize your shop.

Making your e-commerce site gives you the freedom to customize your shop the way you would like it to appear. The significant difference between Shopify or a similar platform Shopify and taking with the "from scratch" method is the level of technical knowledge required. With Shopify, it is unnecessary to have to code to make your website, and you are not responsible for hosting or security as they are covered in the price you pay Shopify. However, you must ensure these are covered with a completely independent website. However, they offer complete freedom, and there's you don't have to worry about whether you'll lose your business if the hosting platform is down.

Promote Your Online Lingerie Business.

If your online lingerie store can be considered an expansion of the physical store, then you can make sure to promote your online store at your physical store. It is possible to do these using banners and flyers advertising your online store in conjunction with the store. You can also do this with exclusive promotions only available in-store, such as 15% off your customers' next purchase online when they spend more than $50 at the shop. If you own physical space, it is most likely that digital marketing is the most efficient way to advertise your company. If you're not proficient enough to promote your business on your own, you should partner with an online marketing firm to get your company's name and your products in the eyes of thousands of prospective buyers.

The E-Business Risks.

E-business is an electronic type of business carried out over the Internet. The business model has grown in popularity since technology has advanced, with smaller and better computers. Today, many businesses run their business solely on the Internet and will never have a brick-and-mortar shopfront. While e-businesses are easy to establish and require only a tiny amount of in the way of capital investment, but they are still susceptible to the usual risks that all businesses face.

Systematic Risk.

Systematic risk is the threat an organization is exposed to from the whole market or market segment within which it is operating. One classic instance of systematic risk within the e-business industry is the dot-com collapse of 2000-2001. Many e-businesses were founded with a public offering, then were acquired by other online companies. Most of these e-businesses did not have enough cash flow and could not make profits. These companies focused on growth over stability, which led to an unsustainable economic bubble bursting, ruining several dot-com firms. While this kind of systemic risk will not happen repeatedly, most market segments will be in cycles of business expanding before slowing down and eventually regaining. Entrepreneurs and owners of online businesses should be aware of their market segment and devise a plan for each business cycle phase.

Security Risk.

E-businesses are exposed to various types of risks related to customers' information and business data security. Hackers and computer viruses are always trying to hack into online businesses and take customer identities and financial details. It poses security risks that force online businesses to utilize encryption software and codes that restrict an outsider's capability to penetrate their secure systems. The security risks associated with online transactions can cause legal problems for online businesses since they must safeguard consumers' privacy under federal and state laws. Any breach in an e-commerce security system can also raise the risk for insurance because insurance companies demand more significant premiums for businesses with legal problems, should they choose to accept the e-business as a customer.

Corporate Risk.

Risks for business are the risks companies face when operating business activities daily. It includes the cost of inventory, labor, overhead, or supply chain issues. Most online businesses don't have massive warehouses or physical locations and must rely on a supply chain in transporting goods to customers. If a company must depend on other companies to distribute products, risk can increase. Business risk also increases when an online business cannot buy and get its inventory through supply chains swiftly and effectively.

Questions for Entrepreneurs.

Beginning your entrepreneurial journey towards "being your boss" is an exciting prospect. Alongside all your research, be sure you research regarding your situation and the job you're in.

Some questions to ask yourself.

- Do I have the character or temperament to take on the world according to my terms?
- Have I got the atmosphere and the resources to commit all my energy to my business?
- Do I have a plan for exit in place with a clear timeframe if my venture doesn't work?
- Am I able to create a clear plan for the coming "x" amount of time? Or will I encounter challenges midway due to financial, family, and other commitments? Have I a plan of action or a mitigation plan to deal with those obstacles?
- Have I got the network to get assistance and guidance when needed?
- Am I able to identify constructed bridges with mentors with experience to gain insight from their experience?
- Have I completed the draft of a full risk analysis, including the dependence on external variables?
- Have I considered the value of my offer and how it can be placed in the market?
- If my product is replacing an already existing item on the market, what will my competitors react?

- To protect my offer, Is it sensible to obtain a patent? Have I the ability to commit the time?
- Do I have a clear idea of my primary customers for the initial phase? Do I have plans for scalability prepared for expanding into larger markets?
- Have I identified the sales as well as distribution routes?

Questions that go beyond External Factors:

- Does my venture comply with local laws and regulations? If it's not feasible locally, could I, and should I move to another area?

- What is the time frame to get the permit or authorization required by the appropriate authorities? Am I able to have the stamina to last this time?

- Have I got a plan to acquire the staff and resources? Do I have cost considerations for this?
- What are the timelines to bring the prototype to market or for the services to become operational?
- Who are my main clients?
- What are the sources of funding I might need to talk to for this to be successful? Does my idea have enough merit to attract the attention of potential investors?
- What is the technical infrastructure I require?
- After the company is established, Will I have the money to increase this to the next stage?

Are other significant firms likely to take my idea and destroy my company?

Conclusion:

According to Merriam-Webster's definition of an entrepreneur, it is *"one who plans and manages the risk of running an enterprise or business."* They often have to take on more risk than the typical businessperson and may reap greater rewards. Economists recognize entrepreneurship as a vital resource for production. Entrepreneurs utilize land, work, and capital to contribute to the economy by providing products and services. Entrepreneurs create an outline of the business plan for most new projects, which spells out the necessary resources to hire, finance, and the new company's direction. Capital funding is often difficult for entrepreneurs just starting their ventures, so they usually start small and invest their funds in the project. Some entrepreneurs launch projects independently and take on the risk-to-reward ratio without assistance. Some, however, look for partnerships. With the benefits of more financial resources and credit, businesses tend to expand faster and achieve tremendous success.

There is no requirement to run your entire business on the Internet to take advantage of business opportunities online. Small-scale businesses may just require an email address to communicate with their customers, clients, and suppliers via email. Some companies may also use their website for their entire operations online. The many advantages of online businesses include:

- worldwide access, all day, seven days, seven days
- better client service by providing more flexibility
- cost savings
- quicker delivery of goods
- greater professionalism
- fewer paper wastes
- chances to manage the business of your choice from anywhere around the globe.

Customers may choose to visit your website to learn more about your offerings and services rather than visit you in person. They should also look up your website's address and your email address on business cards and other promotional material. **Entrepreneurs are the ones who create jobs that are companies design every product or service we utilize regularly.**

Series: Wealth 2022
1. Online Entrepreneurship.
2. Starting Your Own Business
3. Wealth Management
4. Passive Income.

www.ingramcontent.com/pod-product-compliance
Lightning Source LLC
Chambersburg PA
CBHW070251220526
45465CB00004B/1579